HAMSTERS

MICHAELA MILLER

Contents

Heinemann Library
Chicago, Illinois

Wild Ones

Wild hamsters live in **deserts**. They sleep underground in **burrows** during the day to keep out of the sun. At night, the desert cools down and hamsters come out to search for food.

wild hamster

The most common pet hamster is the golden hamster. All pet golden hamsters came from one golden hamster family found in the Syrian desert in 1930. This is why they are also called Syrian hamsters.

HAMSTER FACT

Hamsters store food in pouches in their cheeks.

3

The Hamster for You

Golden hamsters like to be alone. If you put two in one cage they would probably fight and kill each other. Chinese or Russian hamsters will not do this if they get used to each other when they are very young.

Russian hamster

HAMSTER FACT

Long-haired hamsters need **grooming** every other day.

Hamsters are naturally very active at night and sleepy during the day. It is unkind to keep disturbing your hamster during the day.

Where to Find Your Hamster

A veterinarian may be able to give you the name of a local hamster **breeder**. **Animal shelters** are often looking for good homes for hamsters. You may even have a relative or friend who has some hamster babies.

When you go to get your hamster, take a box with holes in it, so that the hamster has some air.

HAMSTER FACT

Hamsters live for about two or three years.

A Healthy Hamster

Choose a plump hamster with soft, glossy fur. Its skin should be free of any sore patches, cuts, pimples, and rashes. Its eyes, nose, ears, mouth, and bottom should be clean.

Hamsters can catch colds and flu from people.

A hamster crouching in a corner of the cage is probably not very healthy.

Safe Hands

Your hamster may not be very tame at first. It may try to wriggle away. Start taming your hamster in the evening when it is likely to be awake.

Put some food in its cage and tap the front lightly to attract the hamster's attention. When it moves forward, hand it some food and pet it gently.

After a week, try lifting the hamster in the palms of both your hands. Do not hold the hamster more than eight inches above the ground.

HAMSTER FACT

Hamsters will jump out of your hands if they are frightened. It is important to move slowly and quietly.

Feeding Time

A good pet supply store will have the right mixture of grains, seeds, and nuts for hungry hamsters. Hamsters also like fresh fruits and vegetables, like apples, pears, tomatoes, lettuce, and carrots.

HAMSTER FACT

Rhubarb leaves, potato tops, tomato leaves and spinach will poison your hamster.

Feed your hamster once a day, usually in the early evening. Put the food in a heavy dish so that it can't tip over. Attach a **drip-fed water bottle** to the side of the cage and keep it full of fresh water.

13

Home Sweet Home

Hamsters are very busy animals, so their home should be as big as possible. A ten gallon aquarium with a strong wire mesh lid is a good home for one hamster. There should be a nest box inside with soft hay or **bedding**.

Hamsters need lots of exercise, so fix a solid wheel - available from pet supply stores - to the cage wall. The cage should be somewhere warm but out of direct sunlight and drafts.

 Hamsters need a hardwood **gnawing block** to wear down their teeth.

Keeping Clean

Put a layer of coarse sawdust, wood shavings, or wood chips in the cage. Every week clean the cage thoroughly and put in fresh **bedding**.

Russian hamsters

HAMSTER FACT

Newspaper and magazine print is poisonous to your hamster. Do not use this to line the cage.

Take away hamster droppings and uneaten food every day. At first move some of the **urine**-soaked sawdust to the same corner every day, away from your hamster's food. It will soon use this area as its bathroom.

17

At the Veterinarian

Hamsters are very healthy animals if they are looked after correctly. If your hamster seems to be sick, take it to a veterinarian immediately. Small animals can get very sick, very quickly.

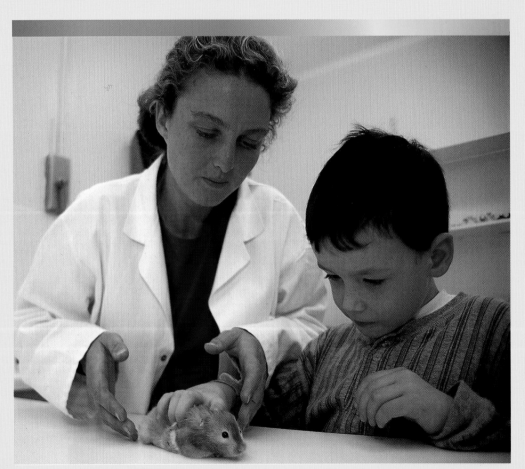

If your hamster's breathing seems strange and its eyes get cloudy, it may not be healthy. Sore spots on its skin or damp patches around its bottom are also bad signs, so see a veterinarian immediately.

HAMSTER FACT

If your hamster gets too cold, it may hibernate and look as if it is dead. Warm it in your hands before you worry.

19

No More Babies

It is not a good idea to let your hamster have babies. A female hamster usually has between five and seven young in each **litter**. Within two months each hamster needs its own cage, otherwise they will fight.

HAMSTER FACT

It takes sixteen days for a baby hamster to grow inside its mother.

If your hamster gives birth, leave the mother and babies completely alone, except at feeding time. Ask your veterinarian for advice.

baby hamsters—seven days old

A Note From the ASPCA

Pets are often our good friends for the very best of reasons. They don't care how we look, how we dress, or who our friends are. They like us because we are nice to them and take care of them. That's what being friends is all about.

This book has given you information to help you know what your pet needs. Learn all you can from this book and others, and from people who know about animals, such as veterinarians and workers at animal shelters like the ASPCA. You will soon become your pet's most important friend.

MORE BOOKS TO READ

Dudek, Isabella. *House Pets*. Milwaukee: Gareth Stevens, 1995.

Gutman, Bill. *Becoming Best Friends With Your Hamster, Guinea Pig, or Rabbit*. Brookfield, Conn.: Millbrook 1997.

Glossary

When words in this book are in bold, **like this**, they are explained in this glossary.

animal shelters There are lots of these shelters all around the country that look after unwanted pets and try to find them new homes.

bedding Coarse sawdust or wood chips are put into a hamsters cage so it can burrow and dig.

breeder People who raise and sell animals are called breeders.

burrows These are underground holes and tunnels used by some animals.

desert Deserts are dry, sandy and rocky places in the world where there are very few trees and plants.

drip-fed water bottle This is a bottle that is specially made so that the water comes out drip by drip.

gnawing block This is a hardwood block for a hamster to chew on to wear down its teeth.

grooming This is gently brushing your hamster.

litter Hamster babies are born in groups called litters.

urine This is the name for liquid body waste.

Index

Published by Heinemann Interactive Library, an imprint of Reed Educational & Professional Publishing,
Chicago, IL
Visit our website at www.heinemannlibrary.com
© 1998 RSPCA

Customer Service 1-888-454-2279

Printed in Hong Kong / China
Designed by Nicki Wise and Lisa Nutt
Illustrations by Michael Strand
02 01
10 9 8 7 6 5 4 3

The Library of Congress has cataloged the hardcover version of this
book as follows:

Library of Congress Cataloging-in-Publication Data
Miller, Michaela, 1961-
    Hamsters / Michaela Miller.
        p. cm. — (Pets)
    Includes bibliographical reference and index.
    Summary: A simple introduction to choosing and caring for
hamsters.
    ISBN 1-57572-576-2 (lib. bdg.)
    1. Hamsters as pets — Juvenile literature. [1. Hamsters.
2. Pets.] 1. Title. II. Series: Miller, Michaela. 1961- Pets.
SF459.H3M55 1998   97-11984
636.9'356—dc21   CIP
                                                       AC

Acknowledgments
The author and publishers are grateful to the following for permission to reproduce copyright photographs
Ardea/ pp6, 16, 20 John Daniels, 21 I R Beames; Dave Bradford pp3, 7, 8, 10-12, 15, 17; Bruce Coleman/
p2 Jane Burton OSF/ p5 G I Bernard, p9 Zig Leszczynski; RSPCA/pp18, 19 Tim Sambrook
Cover photographs reproduced with permission of: RSPCA
With special thanks to the ASPCA and their consultant Dr. Stephen Zawistowski, who approved the contents of this book.
Every effort has been made to contact copyright holders of any material reproduced in this book. Any omissions will be rectified
in subsequent printings if notice is given to the publisher.